WHAT DO YOU KNOW ABOUT

BULLYING

PETE SANDERS

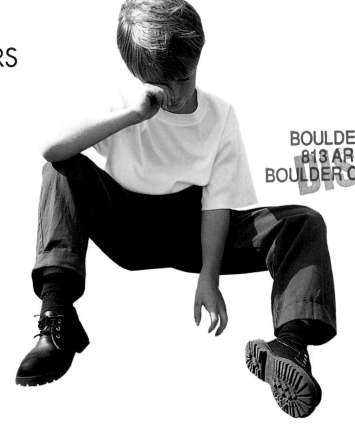

COPPER BEECH BOOKS
BROOKFIELD, CONNECTICUT

Designed and produced by
Aladdin Books Ltd
28 Percy Street
London W1P 0LD

First published in the United States in 1996 by
Copper Beech Books,
an imprint of The Millbrook Press
2 Old New Milford Road
Brookfield, Connecticut 06804

Printed in Belgium

Design   David West Children's
                    Book Design
Designer   Keith Newell
Editor   Jen Green
Picture research   Emma Krikler

Library of Congress Cataloging-in-Publication Data

Sanders, Pete.
Bullying / by Pete Sanders : illustrated by Mike Lacey.
p. cm. -- (What do you know about)
Originally published: London : Watts Book, 1993.
Includes bibliographical references and index.
Summary: Discusses bullying, why it occurs, and how it
can be handled.
ISBN 0-7613-0537-8 (lib. bdg.)
1. Bullying--Juvenile literature. [1. Bullying. 2. Bullies.]
I. Lacey, Mike, ill. II. Title. III. Series: Sanders, Pete.
What do you know about
BF637.B85S36 1996   96-2370
302.3'4--dc20   CIP AC

CONTENTS

INTRODUCTION

SOMETIMES PEOPLE TRY TO PRETEND THAT BULLYING DOESN'T EXIST. IT CAN BE HARD TO FACE UP TO BEING BULLIED. IT CAN ALSO BE DIFFICULT TO UNDERSTAND THE EFFECT BULLYING HAS ON PEOPLE.

People who are being bullied react in different ways.
They might become quiet and moody. Or they may appear nervous and depressed. They might even pretend to be ill, to try to avoid the bully.
  Reading this book will help you learn more about bullying. Each chapter introduces an aspect of bullying. Storylines highlight problem areas, and different ways of dealing with bullying are suggested. This book will help to explain why bullying happens, and what can be done to stop it.

THAT'S IT. THEY'VE GONE TOO FAR.

WHAT IS BULLYING ?

YOU MAY ALREADY HAVE A GOOD IDEA ABOUT WHAT BULLYING MEANS. YOU MAY HAVE BEEN BULLIED YOURSELF. YOU MAY EVEN HAVE BULLIED OTHERS. IT SEEMS TO HAPPEN EVERYWHERE, AND TO LOTS OF PEOPLE.

There are many different kinds of bullying.
Bullies might use words, or they might hurt others physically. Sometimes they demand money or property. You probably know bullies who have tried to take friends away from people and make them feel alone. Bullies will often pick on somebody who will not fight back, or who they think will not tell anyone about them.
  Sometimes bullies say they are "just teasing" or "just playing" to try to excuse what they are doing. Remember that any kind of action which causes hurt or upset in others is serious, and should not be allowed to continue.

Some people don't always take bullying as seriously as they should. Sometimes this is because they don't know exactly what is happening.

△ Wayne Fisher had a reason for arriving at school early. Glancing around the playground, he spotted Nigel and called him over.

THIS IS THE LAST TIME I CAN DO THIS.

WE'LL SEE ABOUT THAT.

Once he had the money, Wayne headed for the school building. Nobody was allowed in before nine o'clock, so he knew the building would be empty. He needed a quiet place where he could count the money from Nigel.

I HOPE IT'S ENOUGH.

WHOEVER'S IN HERE HAD BETTER COME OUT NOW.

As Wayne counted the money, he heard footsteps outside.

Wayne knew he would need a good excuse for having so much money.

5

◁ Wayne had spent the morning worrying about what excuse he could give the principal, Miss Bass. But she had an unexpected visitor.

MOM, WHAT ARE YOU DOING HERE?

I'LL TELL HER MY MOM GAVE IT TO ME TO BUY A PRESENT FOR GRANDMA'S BIRTHDAY.

Wayne knew he shouldn't tell the truth.

▽ Wayne refused to say anything. Miss Bass decided to keep the money with her until he told the truth. She told Wayne she would see him later.

20 minutes later....

YOUR MOM AND I ARE STILL WAITING TO HEAR WHERE YOU GOT THE MONEY FROM, AND WHAT YOU WANT IT FOR.

Wayne dreaded telling Kevin Stone why he didn't have the money. After all, today was the deadline.

BULLIES OFTEN CHOOSE PLACES WHERE ADULTS WON'T SEE THEM.

Possible danger areas might be: the school bathrooms, the playground, the streets outside school, or on the school stairs. You might be able to think of other places where bullying happens.

BULLIES USUALLY PICK ON SOMEBODY WHO WILL NOT FIGHT BACK.

A bully might:
- push you around.
- call you names.
- hurt you by fighting with you.
- make fun of you and your family.
- talk about you behind your back.
- try to get money from you.
- threaten you in different ways.
- damage or steal your property.
- try to make you do something you don't want to.
- influence others not to be your friend.
- make sexist or racist comments about you or your friends.

WHY DO PEOPLE BECOME BULLIES?

BULLIES LIKE TO BE POWERFUL. SOMETIMES THEY MAY BE JEALOUS OF OTHERS, AND USE BULLYING AS A WAY OF GETTING AT THEM. BULLIES WILL PICK ON ANYONE IF THEY THINK THEY CAN GET AWAY WITH IT. THEY WILL LOOK FOR SITUATIONS WHICH ALLOW THEM TO DO THIS.

People become bullies for all kinds of reasons.
Some people have very fixed ideas about what bullies are like. You know that they are not just bigger boys making trouble. Some may be copying something that is happening to them at home – after all, adults can be bullies too. Or it might be their way of trying to look important in front of others.

Often people who are being bullied will bully others.
This can lead to a kind of "chain" of bullying. You may know of people who bully younger brothers or sisters because they feel helpless in other situations, where they think they do not have any power.

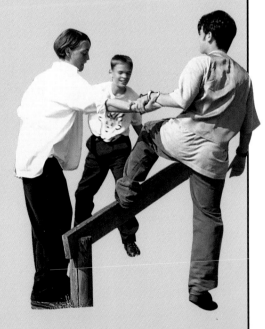

It's not always easy to spot a bully.

WE DON'T NEED WIMPS LIKE YOU IN OUR GANG. YOU'RE DEAD IF YOU EVER TELL.

△ Wayne tried to explain what had happened, but Kevin was even more angry when he found out why Wayne did not have the money.

△ Kevin was furious. Wayne had been avoiding him all day. Now he was determined to find out why Wayne had spent so much time in the office.

▷ Kevin told the gang that Wayne had been caught. Soon they were making up stories about him.

The next day.....

LET'S CALL HIM WAYNE THE PAIN.

THAT'S A GOOD ONE, KEV.

A week later.....

WHY WON'T YOU TELL ME WHAT IS BOTHERING YOU WAYNE?

IF ONLY I COULD TELL SOMEONE THE TRUTH.

△ Wayne's mom was convinced that he was pretending to be ill to avoid having to go to school.

◁ Wayne still hadn't told his mom about Kevin. He had become very moody. But he wasn't able to fool his mom for long. Now he dreaded going to school.

What do you think the truth is?
Do you think Wayne should tell someone?
How do you feel about Kevin?

Being bullied can make you feel very alone.
Some people lie about being bullied. You might even blame yourself, and believe you deserve to be bullied. You may also be forced to do things you don't want to do, such as stealing, and this often makes you feel much worse. Nobody should have to put up with feeling lonely and guilty in this way.

Bullies use fear as a weapon.
Some bullies use force to frighten people into doing what they want. Others use less obvious methods. They may threaten not to be your friend, or let you be part of their gang. All bullies have one thing in common: They rely on people not telling on them.

STANDING UP TO BULLIES

YOU MAY HAVE HEARD GROWN-UPS SAY THAT IT IS IMPORTANT TO STAND UP TO BULLYING. CHALLENGING A BULLY CAN SEEM VERY DIFFICULT, BUT ONCE YOU GIVE IN TO A BULLY'S DEMANDS IT CAN BE HARD TO STOP.

There are several ways to deal with bullying.
It is important to judge each situation carefully. Sometimes it's right to stand up for yourself, and refuse to do what the bully is demanding. At other times, it may be best to leave a situation. Once bullies think they cannot exert power over you, they will probably back down and not pester you again.

Some people will tell you to deal with bullies by appearing confident, or by ignoring the situation and staying out of danger areas. It is up to you to decide when to do this, and when to deal with the problem in a different way.

Judge situations carefully, and don't allow yourself to be forced to do anything you are not happy with.

I HOPE I'M WRONG ABOUT THIS.

I THINK WE NEED TO HAVE A LONG TALK WAYNE.

◁ Mrs. Fisher had noticed that some money had disappeared from her bag. She had decided to leave some money on the table, to see what would happen.

Wayne was caught red-handed.

I CAN'T TELL YOU WHO THEY ARE MOM. THEY'D BEAT ME UP IF I DID.

△ Wayne told his mom that he was being bullied, and that he had been given one last chance to be in the gang.

PLEASE DON'T TELL ANYBODY. IT'LL BE A LOT WORSE FOR ME AT SCHOOL.

Wayne was sorry for stealing the money. He felt guilty, and blamed himself for what was happening.

IF MOM COMES TO SCHOOL THEY'LL KNOW I'VE TOLD ON THEM

Wayne was glad he had told his mom, but he spent that night worrying about what would happen next.

What do you think Wayne's mom will do?

12

TALKING TO PEOPLE CAN HELP.

It is important to know that from time to time you will meet situations which you cannot handle alone. Not talking to someone can often make the situation feel much worse. You may be afraid to say anything because it looks as if you are telling lies. If you are being bullied, talking to somebody about it is not "telling lies." No one deserves to be bullied.

TELLING THE RIGHT PERSON.

Some adults or friends will be better able to help than others. If you are being bullied, it is worth thinking carefully about who to tell. This might be a favorite teacher, or a parent.

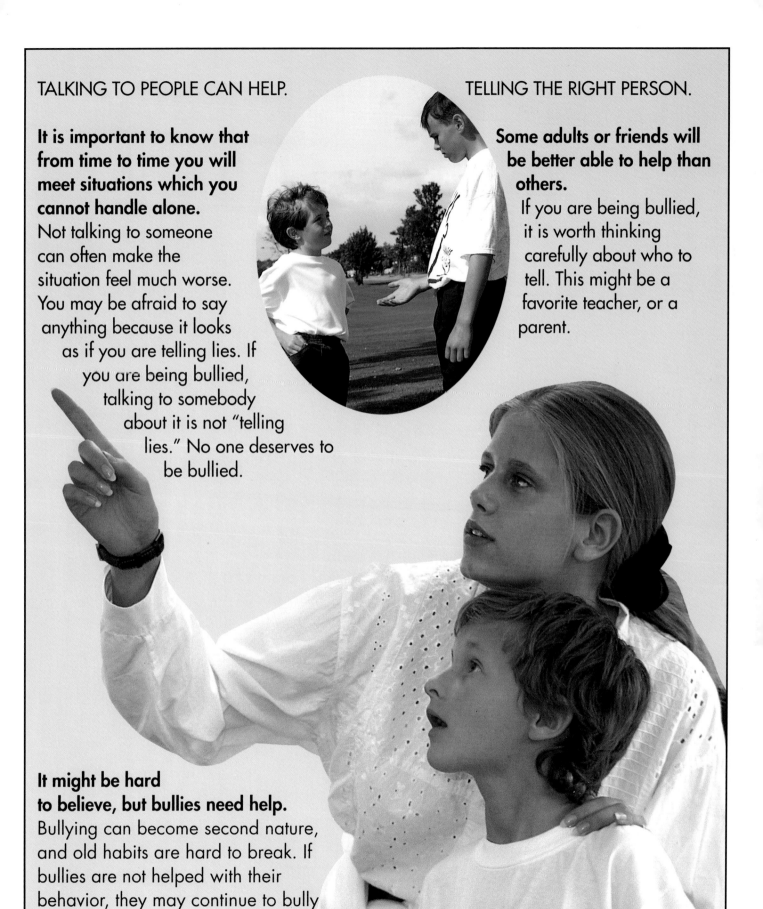

It might be hard to believe, but bullies need help. Bullying can become second nature, and old habits are hard to break. If bullies are not helped with their behavior, they may continue to bully all their lives.

WHAT WILL HAPPEN TO ME IF I TELL?

WHEN SOMETHING GOES WRONG, MOST PEOPLE TRY TO WORK THINGS OUT FOR THEMSELVES. BULLIES RELY ON THIS. THEY KNOW THAT IT IS OFTEN DIFFICULT TO TELL OTHERS, AND THIS IS PARTICULARLY TRUE AS YOU GET OLDER.

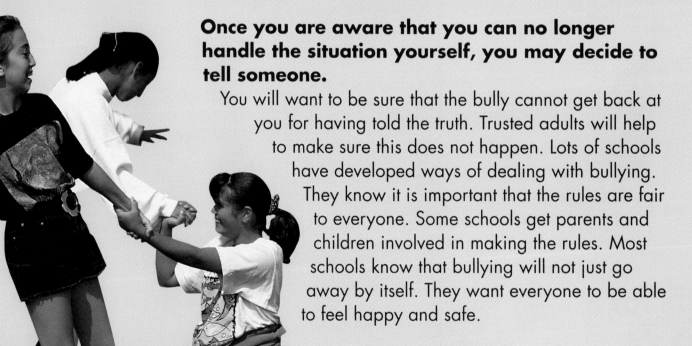

Once you are aware that you can no longer handle the situation yourself, you may decide to tell someone.

You will want to be sure that the bully cannot get back at you for having told the truth. Trusted adults will help to make sure this does not happen. Lots of schools have developed ways of dealing with bullying. They know it is important that the rules are fair to everyone. Some schools get parents and children involved in making the rules. Most schools know that bullying will not just go away by itself. They want everyone to be able to feel happy and safe.

Bullying can happen everywhere. Most schools will try to help people to deal with bullying for themselves.

The following day....

THANK YOU. I'LL BE THERE AT TEN-THIRTY

△ Wayne was pleased that his mom had agreed to see Miss Bass when everyone would be in class. He was still feeling very nervous.

Miss Bass talked to Mrs. Fisher for a long time about what the school did about bullies.

I PROMISE WE WON'T SINGLE WAYNE OUT.

△ Miss Bass said she would find out who was responsible.

IT'S A LOVELY DAY OUT THERE. THE FRESH AIR WILL DO YOU GOOD.

Because he had no money for Kevin, Wayne tried to stay in at recess. When he couldn't, he tried to stay close to the teacher on duty.

I COULDN'T GET ANYTHING FOR YOU. MOM'S EVEN STOPPED MY ALLOWANCE.

Wayne expected to be beaten up. Instead Kevin called him names, and made fun of his family.

I TOLD YOU SO. HE'S NOT WORTH WASTING TIME ON.

How do you think Wayne feels?

15

A few days later.....

I CAN'T BELIEVE I WAS SO CONCERNED ABOUT BEING IN KEVIN'S GANG. THEY'RE ALWAYS IN TROUBLE.

◁ Wayne was making new friends from another class.

LET'S SEE YOU BEG FOR IT.

▽ Wayne watched as Kevin and his gang played their usual tricks. He felt really sorry for Nigel.

▷ Wayne decided to tell Miss Bass. She would listen to him and be fair.

THAT'S IT. THEY'VE GONE TOO FAR.

I'M REALLY PLEASED YOU CAME WAYNE. I KNOW IT COULDN'T HAVE BEEN EASY.

What do you think Miss Bass will do?

16

Most grown-ups will try to help you to stand up for yourself.
A few adults think that bullying and being bullied are a part of growing up. Most do not. You have the right to say no to someone who is bothering you.

Adults cannot always tell that you are being bullied, even if it feels obvious to you.
It is not "telling tales" to discuss your problem with someone. Bottling things up can make things worse.

Sometimes the idea of belonging to a gang is actually more exciting than the reality.
You may think you are missing out on something by not being in the gang. This is not always true.

HOW DO SCHOOLS DEAL WITH BULLYING?

MOST ADULTS AGREE THAT BULLYING IS WRONG, AND THEY REALIZE HOW DIFFICULT IT CAN BE TO TELL THE TRUTH ABOUT BEING BULLIED. THEY ALSO KNOW HOW IMPORTANT IT IS TO TRY TO PROTECT THE PERSON WHO IS BEING BULLIED.

Bullies must be helped to understand the effect of their behavior on other people, and how it makes those people feel.

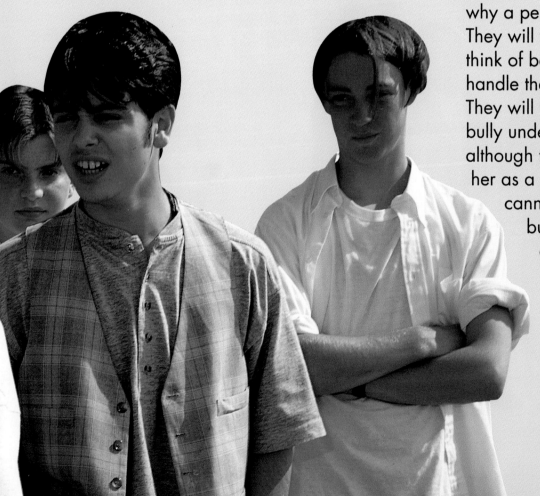

Adults will try to find out why a person is bullying. They will want bullies to think of better ways to handle their feelings. They will try to help the bully understand that, although they like him or her as a person, they cannot allow the bullying to continue.

Everyone has the right to enjoy life without being threatened or made to feel small. Everyone needs to feel cared for and protected.

△ After questioning everyone for a long time, Miss Bass knew that Kevin was the leader.

▷ Miss Bass talked to Kevin for over half an hour.

◁ Kevin told Miss Bass his mom was always busy with his new baby sister, and his dad was hardly ever there.

▽ Miss Bass now understood a little more about Kevin's bullying. She knew that habits like this were hard to break.

IT'S YOUR FAULT. I'LL GET THE BLAME FOR THIS.

◁ This time, Wayne did not try to avoid Kevin. Although he was nervous, he felt strong enough to stand up to him.

▽ Wayne understood Kevin more now, and actually felt sorry for him.

GO AHEAD AND TRY. YOU'RE NOT SO BIG WITHOUT YOUR GANG TO BACK YOU UP.

The next day was the last day of school before the summer vacation.

I'M REALLY SORRY.

Wayne felt badly about having bullied Nigel.

◁ Kevin did not chase after him. Wayne felt pleased with himself for standing up to Kevin.

▽ He wanted to make it up to Nigel if he could.

IF ANY OF THEM PICK ON YOU AGAIN, JUST LET ME KNOW.

IS IT OKAY TO BE IN A GANG?

Being part of a group can be a lot of fun.
It's great to share good times together, and lots of people enjoy the feeling of confidence that joining in with others can give them.

But gangs can encourage bullying.
There are times when gang members go along with ideas, not because they want to, but because they are afraid of being bullied if they refuse. By simply allowing bullying to happen, the other members of the gang become bullies too.

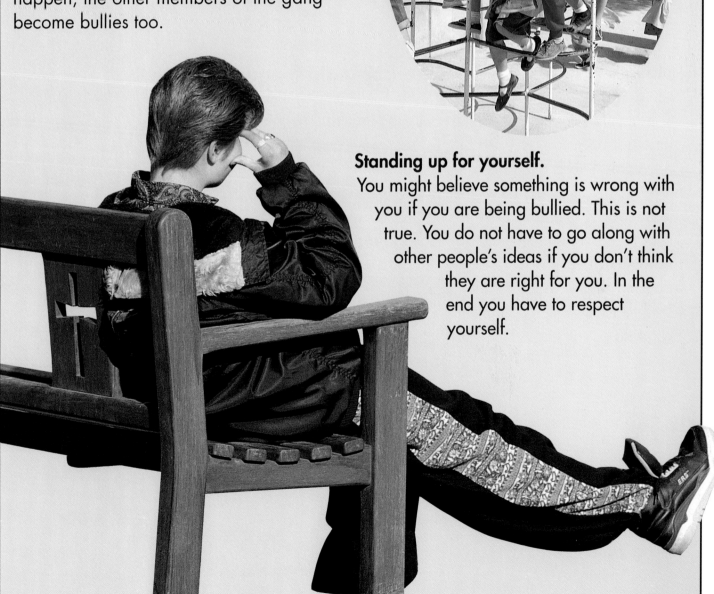

Standing up for yourself.
You might believe something is wrong with you if you are being bullied. This is not true. You do not have to go along with other people's ideas if you don't think they are right for you. In the end you have to respect yourself.

WHY DO SOME PEOPLE GET PICKED ON MORE THAN OTHERS?

YOU MAY HAVE THOUGHT ABOUT HOW DIFFICULT IT IS FOR NEW PEOPLE TO FIT IN. THEY MAY NOT KNOW ANYONE. IT CAN BE HARD TO MAKE NEW FRIENDS, PARTICULARLY IF THE REST OF THE CLASS KNOW EACH OTHER WELL.

Newcomers are sometimes missing old friends and familiar situations.
They could well be feeling nervous and unsure. They might even behave in unexpected ways because of this. You may have known newcomers who even bully others, or join in with bullying to become accepted by a particular group. Some schools know about this, and have tried to come up with ideas to support anyone who feels isolated and alone. Many schools are very strict about anyone who is made to feel bad because they come from a different culture.

Some schools have a "buddy system," whereby newcomers are looked after by someone who knows all about the school.

◁ That summer, Wayne went to his grandma's house at the beach. He enjoyed playing with one of her neighbors. Karen always listened to Wayne.

> I WAS REALLY SCARED, BUT I'M GLAD I STOOD UP TO THEM.

Karen's story....

> THIS IS SATNAM, WHO'S STARTING SCHOOL TODAY.

▷ Wayne told Karen all about Kevin and the gang. He was surprised to find out that Karen had been bullied too.

A couple of weeks later....

> YOU WOULDN'T CATCH ANY OF US EATING THAT GARBAGE.

> NONE OF YOU HAVE GIVEN HER A CHANCE.

△ A new girl had started at Karen's school. Lots of the other girls made fun of Satnam.

▷ Karen knew that the girls were being racist. They hadn't even bothered to find out anything about Satnam. It just didn't seem fair.

△ Karen felt annoyed with the others.

Now that Karen and Satnam were friends, the other girls made fun of them both.

Karen and Satnam gradually became friends.

◁ Karen was shocked. She was really annoyed about what the others had done. She spent all weekend thinking about what to do.

That Saturday Karen and Satnam went shopping.

What do you think Karen is going to do?
What would you do?

IT'S NOT ONLY BOYS THAT ARE BULLIES.

You already know that girls can be bullies too.
They sometimes do this in exactly the same way
as boys. Quite often, girls will tease each other,
and call people names. They might try to take
people's friends away and talk about them
behind their backs.

Although it happens most often that boys
bully other boys and girls other girls, it does
not always happen like this.

**Boys usually fight more when they are
bullying.**
Boys think fighting makes them look big in front
of their friends. Some boys think this is what is
expected of them. They may have been told that boys
don't cry.

Many boys do not like to show their real
feelings. But showing your feelings is
not a sign of weakness.
It is a sign of strength.

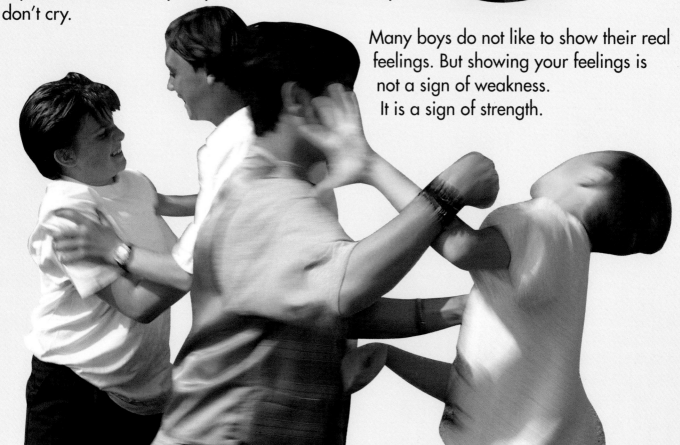

RACIST BULLYING

BULLIES WILL OFTEN PICK ON PEOPLE SIMPLY BECAUSE THEY ARE DIFFERENT IN SOME WAY. IT MAY BE THE KINDS OF CLOTHES THEY WEAR, OR THE FOOD THEY EAT, OR THE NEIGHBORHOOD THEY COME FROM.

Bullies will use all kinds of tactics to hurt people's feelings.
People can be singled out just because they have to wear glasses. Picking on somebody who is a different color is a very common way of bullying. Some people believe they are better than others, just because they are from a different race or culture. Racist bullies will refuse to get to know the person they are bullying, and will concentrate only on the differences they believe exist between them.

People come from all kinds of different backgrounds. If we only look at the differences instead of getting to know the person, we may be missing out on a lot.

WE'VE TRIED TO IGNORE IT, BUT IT'S GETTING OUT OF HAND NOW.

SOMETIMES IGNORING THINGS CAN WORK, BUT NOT ALWAYS.

Later that same week....

HOW DO YOU THINK BULLYING MAKES YOU FEEL?

◁ Karen told her favorite teacher about how the girls were behaving. She knew that this teacher would understand and try to do something about it.

△ The class did some lessons on why people bully, and different ways of handling it.

◁ The teacher organized a mediation session. The girls talked together about what had been happening.

I FEEL REALLY UPSET WHEN THEY MAKE FUN OF HOW I DRESS.

I JOINED IN BECAUSE THE OTHERS WERE DOING IT.

△ Everyone was given a chance to say how they felt. The girls began to realize they hadn't given Satnam a chance.

AND SO WE HAVE DECIDED TO ASK FOR VOLUNTEERS TO LOOK AFTER NEW GIRLS, AND GIRLS WHO ARE BEING BULLIED. WE DON'T WANT ANYONE TO BE UNHAPPY IN OUR SCHOOL.

◁ It took some time. The girls knew they had been racist, and had snubbed Karen too.

BULLYING GOES ON EVERYWHERE. I THINK OUR SCHOOL DID REALLY WELL. WE LEARNED HOW TO DEAL WITH IT FOR OURSELVES.

I WISH WE HAD THE SAME KIND OF THING AT MY SCHOOL. I KNOW A LOT ABOUT BULLYING AND HOW IT FEELS.

△ Things began to get a lot better.

▽ It was the beginning of the new school year. Miss Bass was talking to the students about new beginnings. Wayne had already made up his mind that he would like to help sort out the bullying in his school. He had collected lots of information about where to get help.

That September....

DEALING WITH BULLYING

Schools have developed various ways of dealing with bullying.

School mediation programs give people who are being bullied a chance to talk directly to the bully about their feelings. Bullies also have the chance to talk. A teacher or another adult is on hand to make sure that the meeting is fair, and to help people to talk about ways of solving the problem.

Some schools have a "School Council."
Representatives of each class meet with a teacher to discuss any problems or concerns. It is an opportunity for the students to have their say in what they would like to see happening in the school.

WHAT CAN I DO?

BY NOW YOU KNOW A LOT ABOUT BULLYING, AND PROBABLY HAVE LOTS OF YOUR OWN IDEAS ABOUT HOW TO HANDLE IT. YOU KNOW THAT YOU CAN STOP SOME BULLYING BY IGNORING IT, OR BY BEING CONFIDENT ENOUGH TO SAY NO. IN OTHER SITUATIONS, IT IS BEST TO TELL AN ADULT.

Any kind of bullying that is upsetting you needs to be dealt with. After all, bullying affects everyone, not just bullies and those they are picking on. Those who know about it or who are watching it take place are affected too. You know how bullying can make you feel, and that there are actions you can take to help bullying stop. Sometimes this might be something you do alone; sometimes you will need the help of others. Judging a situation needs careful thought. Above all, you know that you can do something about bullying, even if it is not always easy to believe it at the time.

If you are being bullied, talking to someone is often the first step toward solving the problem.

RESOURCES

BELOW IS A LIST OF ORGANIZATIONS THAT WILL BE ABLE TO HELP IF YOU ARE BEING BULLIED:

Committee For Children
2203 Airport Way S.
Suite 500
Seattle, WA
98134-2027
(800) 634-4449

Defense For Children International
30 Irving Place, 9th Floor
New York, NY
10003
(212) 228-4773

Legal Services For Children
1254 Market St., 3rd Floor
San Francisco, CA
94102
(415) 863-3762

National Alliance For Safe Schools
9344 Lanham Severn Rd.,
No. 104
Lanham, MD
20706
(301) 306-0200

National Association For Mediation in Education
1726 M Street, NW
Suite 500
Washington, DC
20036-4502
(202) 466-2772

National Committee For Prevention of Child Abuse
332 S. Michigan Ave.
Suite 1600
Chicago, IL
60604-4357
(312) 663-3520

National Safe Kids Campaign
111 Michigan Ave. NW
Washington, DC 20010
(202) 884-4993

National School Safety Center
4165 Thousand Oaks Blvd.
Suite 290
Westlake Village, CA
91362
(805) 373-9977

INDEX

Photocredits
Special thanks to Paul Seheult/Eye Ubiquitous for taking all the pictures in this book.
Front cover picture by Roger Vlitos